OUT-OF-THIS-WORLD ALIENS

HIDDEN PICTURE PUZZLES

BY
JILL KALZ

ILLUSTRATED BY
SIMON SMITH

PICTURE WINDOW BOOKS
a capstone imprint

DESIGNER: LORI BYE
ART DIRECTOR: NATHAN GASSMAN
PRODUCTION SPECIALIST: KATHY MCCOLLEY
THE ILLUSTRATIONS IN THIS BOOK WERE CREATED DIGITALLY.

PICTURE WINDOW BOOKS
1710 ROE CREST DRIVE
NORTH MANKATO, MN 56003
WWW.CAPSTONEPUB.COM

LIBRARY OF CONGRESS CATALOGING-IN-PUBLICATION DATA
CATALOGING-IN-PUBLICATION INFORMATION IS ON FILE WITH THE LIBRARY OF CONGRESS.
ISBN 978-1-4048-7942-3 (LIBRARY BINDING)
ISBN 978-1-4048-8076-4 (PAPER OVER BOARD)
ISBN 978-1-4795-1885-2 (EBOOK PDF)

DIRECTIONS:

Look at the pictures and find the items on the lists. Not too tough, right? Not for a clever kid like you. But be warned: The first few puzzles are tricky. The next ones are even trickier. And the final puzzles are for the bravest seekers only. Good luck!

Printed in the United States of America in
North Mankato, Minnesota.
032013   007223CGF13

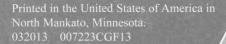

TABLE OF CONTENTS

Happy Birthday!

- cow
- bike
- cupcake
- kitten
- book
- moose

Fútbol Aliençano

- football
- bowling pin
- baseball
- tennis racket
- hockey stick
- volleyball

7

Alien Vacation

- cactus
- starfish
- moon
- hammer
- tomato
- loon

At the Movies

- raccoon
- crow
- bow tie
- newspaper
- banana
- mouse

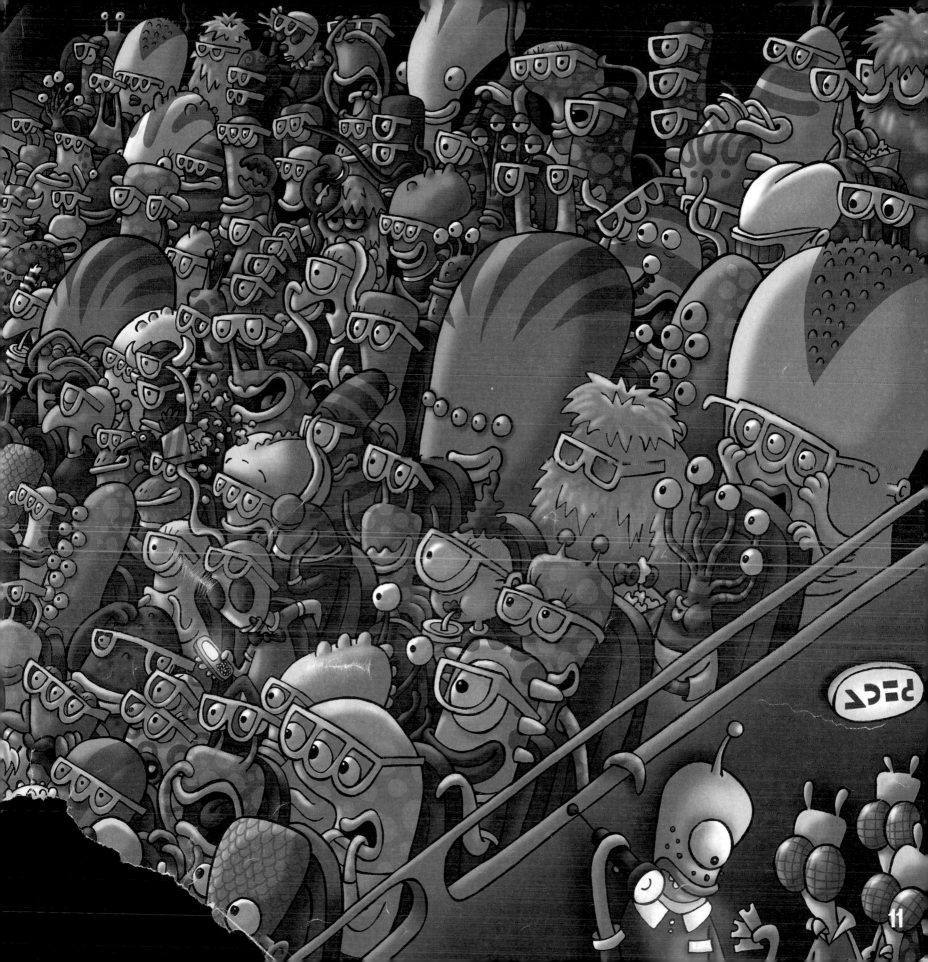

Keep Cool

- candy cane
- lemon
- duck
- polar bear
- Popsicle
- seal
- puppy
- sunscreen
- ice cube

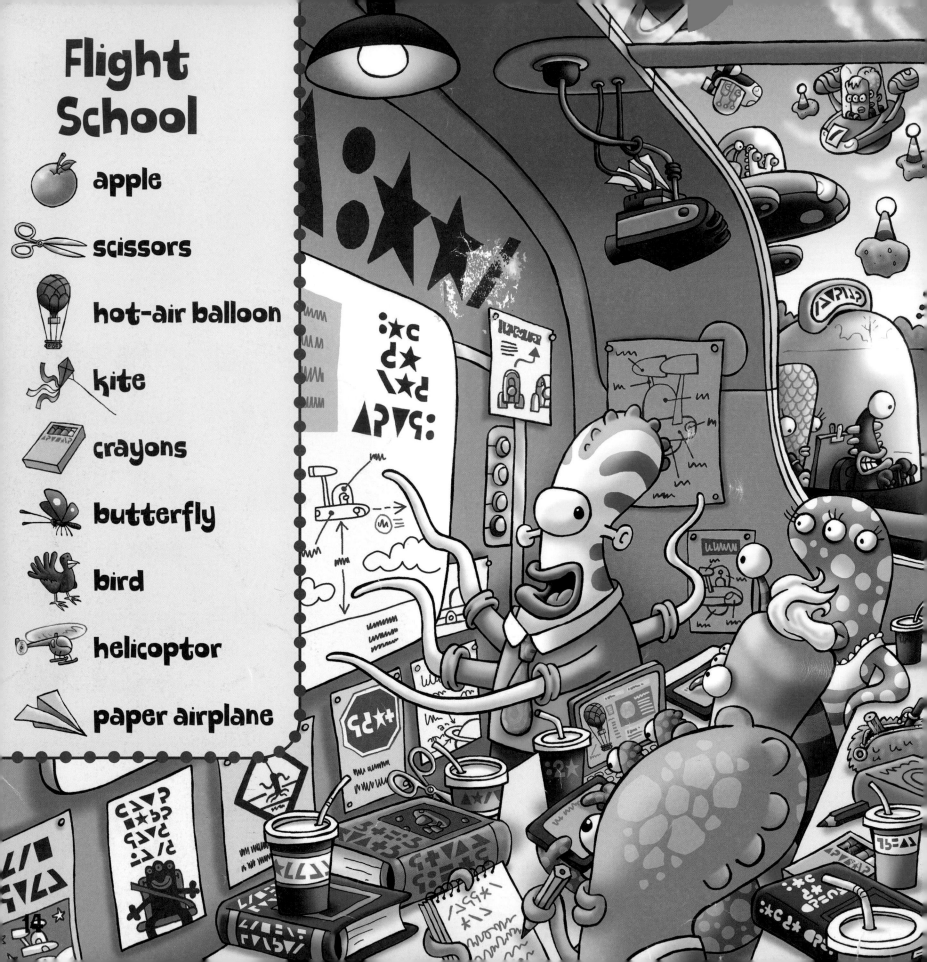

Flight School

- apple
- scissors
- hot-air balloon
- kite
- crayons
- butterfly
- bird
- helicoptor
- paper airplane

Alien Rock Star

- drum
- saxophone
- trombone
- violin
- harmonica
- harp
- flute
- tuba
- trumpet

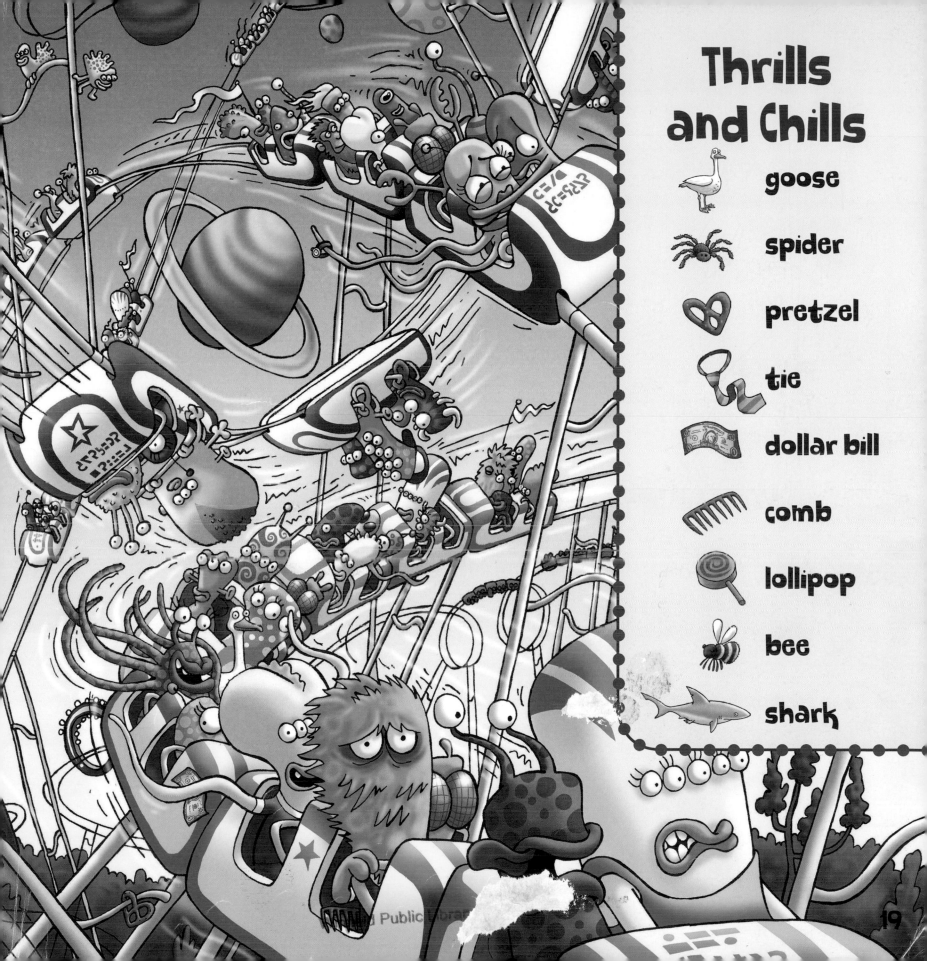

Thrills and Chills

- goose
- spider
- pretzel
- tie
- dollar bill
- comb
- lollipop
- bee
- shark

Get to Work

 rooster

 bagel

 pencil

 picnic basket

 lobster

 soda can

 ant

worm

headphones

Read It

- piggy bank
- wishbone
- toaster
- bull
- whale
-  shell
- spoon
- watermelon
- hummingbird
- igloo
- butterfly
- magnet

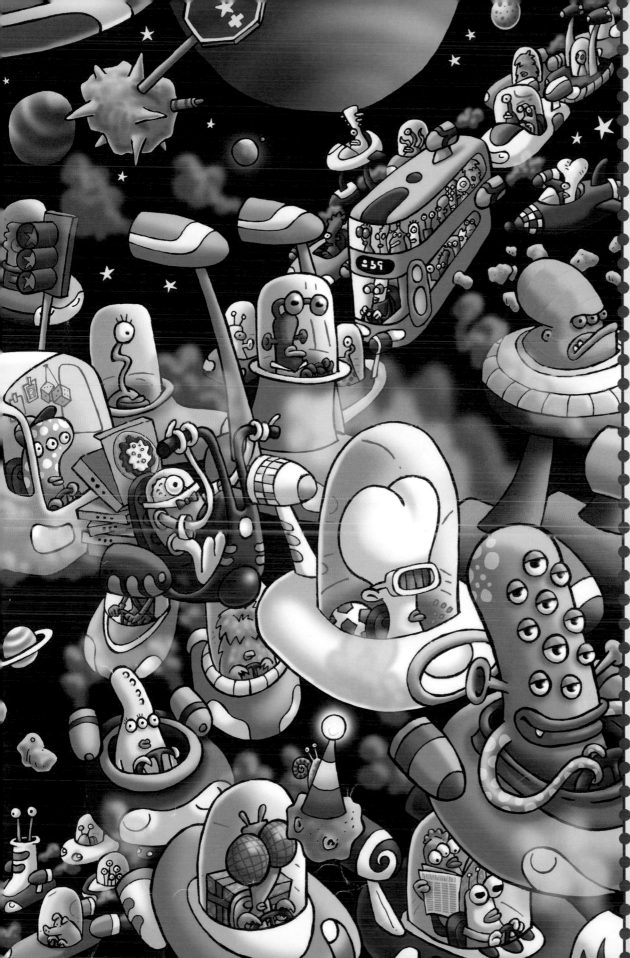

Traffic Jam

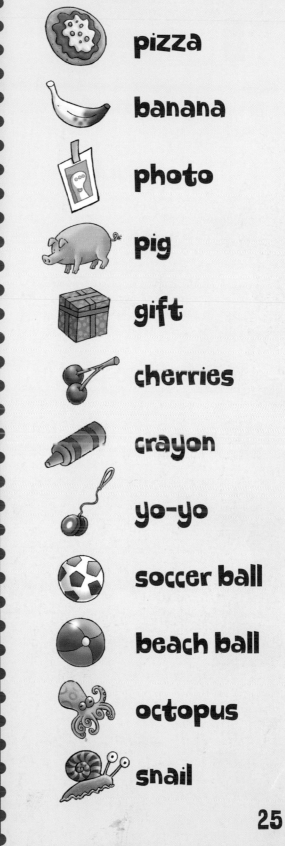

- pizza
- banana
- photo
- pig
- gift
- cherries
- crayon
- yo-yo
- soccer ball
- beach ball
- octopus
- snail

Auto Shop

 stoplight

 juice box

 lightbulb

 Earth

 soup can

license plate

 clock

 flag

 gloves

 old tire

pennant

donut

26

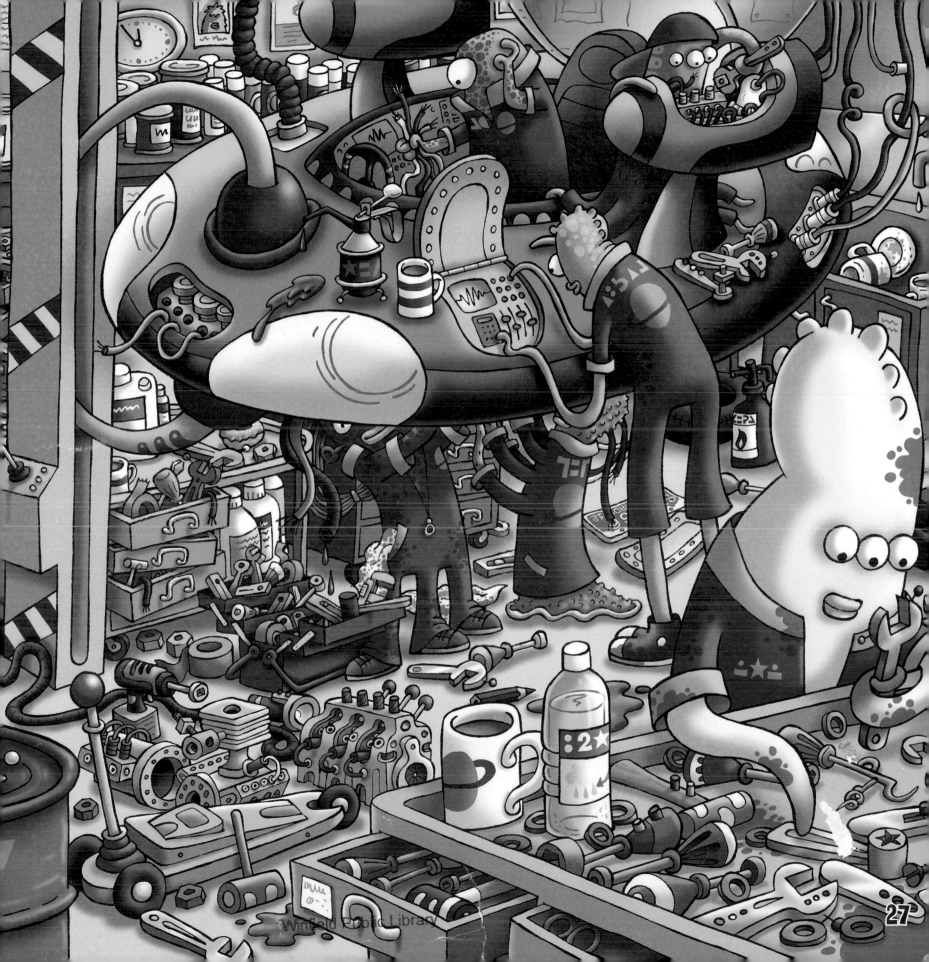

Run!

chicken

stopwatch

tennis ball

lucky clover

turtle

tuba

stamp

teddy bear

clown

broom

playing card

bull

Campout

-  flower
- bug spray
- sailboat
- flashlight
- owl
- toothbrush
- arrow
- hula hoop
- sleeping bag
- camera
- letter
- life ring

SAY WHAT?

FLiP BACK and see if you can decode the alien words!

A	B	C	D	E	F	G	H
I	J	K	L	M	N	O	P	Q
R	S	T	U	V	W	X	Y	Z

Internet Sites

FactHound offers a safe, fun way to find Internet sites related to this book. All of the sites on FactHound have been researched by our staff.

Here's all you do:

Visit *www.facthound.com*

Type in this code: 9781404879423

Check out projects, games and lots more at
www.capstonekids.com

Look for all the books in the series:

CHRISTMAS **CHAOS**

HALLOWEEN **HIDE AND SEEK**

OUT-OF-THIS-WORLD **ALIENS**

Pretty Princess **PARTY**

SCHOOL **SHAKE-UP**

ZOO HIDEOUT